First Facts™

Everyday Character Education

Citizenship

by Janet Riehecky

Consultant:
Madonna Murphy, PhD, Professor of Education
University of St. Francis, Joliet, Illinois
Author, *Character Education in America's Blue Ribbon Schools*

Capstone
press

Mankato, Minnesota

First Facts is published by Capstone Press,
151 Good Counsel Drive, P.O. Box 669, Mankato, Minnesota 56002.
www.capstonepress.com

Library of Congress Cataloging-in-Publication Data
Riehecky, Janet, 1953–
     Citizenship / by Janet Riehecky.
     p. cm. —(First facts. Everyday character education)
     Includes bibliographical references and index.
     ISBN 0-7368-3676-4 (hardcover)
     ISBN 0-7368-5144-5 (paperback)
     1. Citizenship—United States—Juvenile literature. 2. Community life—United States—
Juvenile literature. I. Title. II. Series.
JK1759.R53 2005
323.6'5'0973—dc22   2004012757

Summary: Introduces citizenship through examples of everyday situations where
this character trait can be used.

Editorial Credits
Wendy Dieker, editor; Molly Nei, set designer; Kia Adams, book designer;
     Jo Miller, photo researcher

Photo Credits
Corbis/Ariel Skelley, 20
Gem Photo Studio/Dan Delaney, cover, 1, 5, 6–7, 8, 9, 10–11, 12, 13 (foreground), 19
Photo Courtesy Cathy Wignall/Care Bags Foundation, 15
Photodisc, 13 (background)
Schlesinger Library, Radcliffe College, Harvard University, 16

1 2 3 4 5 6 10 09 08 07 06 05

Table of Contents

Citizenship

Evan and his mom walk home from the store. They see empty cans on the ground. Evan is a good **citizen** and picks up the cans. At home, he puts the cans in a bin for **recycling**. Evan shows good citizenship by making his town a better place to live.

Fun Fact!
Recycling one aluminum soda can saves enough energy to run a television for three hours.

At Your School

Show citizenship at school. Run for class president. Tell classmates how you will make your school a better place.

Voting shows good citizenship. Choose the person who you think will be the best class president.

With Your Friends

Be a good citizen and obey the laws. Wait for the green light before you cross the street. Use the crosswalk and follow the crossing guard's directions.

You and your friends can make your
town a better place. You can **volunteer**
to help fix up parks.

At Home

Remembering people who serve our country makes you a good citizen. Write letters to friends and family members serving in the **armed forces**. Tell them you are proud of them. Thank them for keeping us safe.

> **!** **Fact!**
> You can write a letter to any service member at www.OperationDearAbby.net.

In Your Community

Helping people shows good citizenship. You can help serve meals to people in need.

Learning about history is another way to be a good citizen. Visit historical places. Learn about the lives of people that shaped your **community**.

Annie Wignall

Giving to people in need is a good way to show citizenship. When Annie Wignall was 11 years old, she started the Care Bags Foundation. People give new clothes, toys, and other things to Annie. She sends these things in bags to needy kids around the world.

Fact!
In 2002, Annie received the President's Volunteer Service Award for her work.

Susan B. Anthony

Good citizens speak out for their rights. Susan B. Anthony worked to get U.S. women the right to vote. She gave speeches and wrote letters. Anthony worked for many years to change voting laws. In 1920, U.S. women won the right to vote.

Fact!
Anthony was arrested for trying to vote in 1872. She was fined $100.

What Would You Do?

Evan's school is going to stop having a soccer team. Evan signs a **petition** to say he wants to keep soccer. He speaks out for what he thinks is right.

Casey wants to keep soccer too. But she thinks one name won't make a difference. What can Evan say to get Casey to sign the petition?

Amazing but True!

Even dogs can be good citizens. The American Kennel Club has a 10-part test for dogs. Dogs must show they can sit, stay, and come when called. All dogs that pass get a certificate saying they are "Canine Good Citizens."

Hands On: Write a Letter

Good citizens write letters to their leaders. Citizens can tell their leaders if they think something should change. Citizens can also write a letter saying they like what their leaders do.

What You Need

paper
pencil or pen
envelope
postage stamp

What You Do

1. Think of what you want to tell your mayor, senator, or even the president.
2. Write a message to the leader you have chosen.
3. Fold your letter and place it in an envelope.
4. Place a postage stamp on the front of your envelope. Ask an adult to help you look up the address and mail your letter.

Glossary

armed forces (ARMD FORSS-ez)—the people who work to protect our country

citizen (SIT-i-zuhn)—a member of a city, state, or country

community (kuh-MYOO-nuh-tee)—a group of people who live in the same area

petition (puh-TISH-uhn)—a letter signed by many people asking leaders for a change

recycle (ree-SYE-kuhl)—to make used items into new products; people can recycle items such as glass, plastic, newspapers, and aluminum cans.

volunteer (vol-uhn-TIHR)—to offer to do a job without pay

vote (VOHT)—to make a choice in an election

Read More

Bender, Marie. *Good Citizenship Counts.* Character Counts. Edina, Minn.: Abdo, 2003.

Loewen, Nancy. *We Live Here Too!: Kids Talk About Good Citizenship.* Kids Talk. Minneapolis: Picture Window, 2003.

Salzmann, Mary Elizabeth. *I Am a Good Citizen.* Building Character. Edina, Minn.: Abdo, 2003.

Internet Sites

FactHound offers a safe, fun way to find Internet sites related to this book. All of the sites on FactHound have been researched by our staff.

Here's how:

1. Visit *www.facthound.com*
2. Type in this special code **0736836764** for age-appropriate sites. Or enter a search word related to this book for a more general search.
3. Click on the **Fetch It** button.

FactHound will fetch the best sites for you!

Index